GROUND
BREAKERS

BLACK
MUSICIANS

MUDDY WATERS

by Joyce Markovics

CHERRY LAKE PRESS
Ann Arbor, Michigan

CHERRY LAKE PRESS

Published in the United States of America by Cherry Lake Publishing
Ann Arbor, Michigan
www.cherrylakepublishing.com

Reading Adviser: Beth Walker Gambro, MS, Ed., Reading Consultant, Yorkville, IL
Content Adviser: Michael Kramer, PhD, Music Historian
Book Designer: Ed Morgan

Photo Credits: © Album/Alamy Stock Photo, cover and title page; © Lebrecht Music & Arts/Alamy Stock Photo, 5; Farm Security Administration-Office of War Information Photograph Collection (Library of Congress), 6; Wikimedia Commons/Bobpalez, 7; freepik.com, 8; flickr/Alan Levine, 9; © catwalker/Shutterstock, 10; Wikimedia Commons, 11; © Gijsbert Hanekroot/Alamy Stock Photo, 13; © Phillipe Gras/Alamy Stock Photo 14; © D Guest Smith/Alamy Stock Photo, 15; © Phillipe Gras/Alamy Stock Photo, 16; © Records/Alamy Stock Photo, 17; © Gijsbert Hanekroot/Alamy Stock Photo, 18; © Blueee77/Shutterstock, 19; Odile Noël/Alamy Stock Photo, 21; freepik.com, 22.

Cherry Lake Press is an imprint of Cherry Lake Publishing Group.

Library of Congress Cataloging-in-Publication Data

Names: Markovics, Joyce L., author.
Title: Muddy Waters / Joyce Markovics.
Description: Ann Arbor, Michigan : Cherry Lake Publishing, 2023. | Series:
   Groundbreakers: black musicians | Includes bibliographical references
   and index. | Audience: Grades 4-6
Identifiers: LCCN 2023006542 (print) | LCCN 2023006543 (ebook) | ISBN
   9781668927854 (hardcover) | ISBN 9781668928905 (paperback) | ISBN
   9781668930373 (epub) | ISBN 9781668931851 (pdf) | ISBN 9781668933336
   (kindle edition) | ISBN 9781668934814 (ebook)
Subjects: LCSH: Muddy Waters, 1915-1983—Juvenile literature. | Blues
   musicians—United States—Biography—Juvenile literature.
Classification: LCC ML3930.M92 M37 2023 (print) | LCC ML3930.M92 (ebook)
   | DDC 782.421643092 [B]—dc23/eng/20230210
LC record available at https://lccn.loc.gov/2023006542
LC ebook record available at https://lccn.loc.gov/2023006543

Printed in the United States of America by
Corporate Graphics

Note from publisher: Websites change regularly, and their future contents are outside of our control. Supervise children when conducting any recommended online searches for extended learning opportunities.

CONTENTS

THIS IS MUDDY

The music of Muddy Waters buzzes with energy, feeling, and his Southern roots. This groundbreaker went from being a struggling farm worker to one of the greatest blues musicians of all time. Along the way, he created a new style of music with his electric guitar. Muddy sang from his heart and soul. And people of all skin colors listened. He inspired famous rockers as well as everyday people. And Muddy Waters's rich **legacy** still echoes today.

"I WAS ALWAYS SINGING THE WAY I FELT."
—MUDDY WATERS

Blues musician
Muddy Waters

The blues is an American style of music. It was created by formerly enslaved Black people in the South in the late 1800s. Blues songs are often about life's struggles.

EARLY LIFE

Muddy was named McKinley Morganfield at birth. He was born around April 4, 1915, in the Mississippi Delta. The exact date and place of his birth are unknown. McKinley's father, Ollie, was a **sharecropper** who played the guitar. When McKinley was very young, his mother died.

This is a young sharecropper in the southern United States in the early 1900s. Sharecropping often kept poor Black farmers in debt to white landowners.

McKinley went to live with his grandmother, Della Grant. Her little grandson loved playing in the mud. So she started calling him Muddy. Then as he grew older, he was known as Muddy Waters. Della and Muddy lived in a tiny house on a **plantation**. "Our little house was way back in the country," said Muddy. Growing up in Mississippi was hard. Muddy's grandmother struggled to put enough food on the table.

MUDDY WATERS'S HOUSE

Muddy Waters lived most of his first thirty years in a house on this site, part of the Stovall Plantation. In 1996 the restored house was put on display at the Delta Blues Museum in Clarksdale. Muddy Waters was first recorded here in 1941 by Alan Lomax, who was compiling songs for the Library of Congress. Muddy Waters is known as the king of Chicago blues.

This is the original location of Muddy's house on the Stovall Plantation in Mississippi.

Muddy grew up in the same part of Mississippi as John Lee Hooker. He was another great blues musician.

Muddy's grandmother also worked as a sharecropper. Muddy said, "I went to school, but they didn't give you too much schooling because just as soon as you was big enough, you get to working in the fields." As a child, Muddy spent long hours picking cotton in the hot sun. "They handed me a cotton sack when I was about 8 years old," he said. It was **grueling** work. "I never did like the farm but I was out there with my grandmother," Muddy said.

Muddy and his grandmother worked in a cotton field like this one.

"I WANTED TO DEFINITELY BE A MUSICIAN OR A GOOD PREACHER OR A HECK OF A BASEBALL PLAYER."
—MUDDY WATERS

Muddy grew up surrounded by music—especially music that told stories. When Muddy was still a little kid, he started making his own music. "I was messing around with the harmonica," he said. Muddy played at neighborhood picnics. "But I was 13 before I got a real good note out of it," he said.

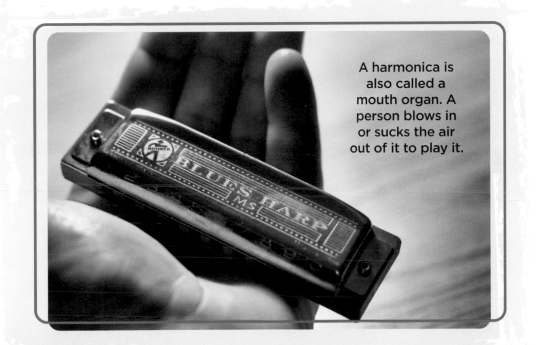

A harmonica is also called a mouth organ. A person blows in or sucks the air out of it to play it.

Muddy grew up in the **segregated** South. There was a system in place that kept white and Black people separate. Black people didn't have the same rights and **opportunities** as white people. And they were mistreated and **terrorized** by some white people.

As a teenager, Muddy taught himself how to play the guitar. To buy his first guitar, "I sold the last horse that we had," Muddy said. He gave the leftover money to Grandma Della. She liked church music. But Muddy loved the Delta blues. This style of music was full of feeling, truth, and the history of the area.

29 USA

BLUES SINGER, 1915-1983

MUDDY WATERS

Muddy's favorite blues guitarists were Robert Johnson and Son House. "That was my **idol**, Son House," Muddy later said. Son was known for playing slide guitar. It had a **distinctive** sound. To get this sound, Son slid a small, hard object across the strings of his guitar while playing. Listening to Son's songs made Muddy's life seem less hard.

Delta blues singer and guitarist, Son House

Robert Johnson was a blues musician and songwriter from the Mississippi Delta. He's been called "the first-ever rock star."

MAKING MUSIC

As a young man, Muddy mastered the guitar. And he came up with a style all his own. Muddy began performing at local clubs and **juke joints**. Yet he still worked as a sharecropper to get by. Then his luck changed. In 1941, a folk music expert named Alan Lomax came to the Mississippi Delta. He was looking for Robert Johnson, hoping to record his music. Instead, Alan found Muddy. Muddy agreed to let Alan record him. After, when Muddy listened to his own songs, he said, "Man, I can sing." A newly confident Muddy left Mississippi to become a blues musician.

"I WANTED TO GET OUT OF MISSISSIPPI IN THE WORST WAY."
—MUDDY WATERS

Muddy enjoyed sharing his love of the blues with listeners.

Muddy's first stop was in Memphis, Tennessee. Then in 1943, he moved north to Chicago, Illinois. Muddy hoped for a better life in the city. Once there, he worked a day job and played clubs at night. But the clubs were noisy. Muddy used an **amplifier** to make his guitar louder. He liked the bold sound. In 1944, Muddy bought his first electric guitar. Using a metal slide, Muddy made his guitar tremble like a human voice.

Muddy plays an electric guitar on stage.

Muddy moved to Chicago during the Great **Migration**. During the 20th century, millions of Black people left the South. They moved to large cities such as Chicago and Detroit with hopes of escaping **racism** and finding better jobs.

Muddy formed a band. Together, they made a new, sound—the Chicago blues. People flocked to hear Muddy's band play. "They say my blues is the hardest blues in the world to play," Muddy once said. And he was right. Few people could play and sing like Muddy. He captured old and new sounds with one guitar slide.

A colorful mural in Chicago featuring Muddy Waters

"MY BLUES ARE SO SIMPLE, BUT SO FEW PEOPLE CAN PLAY IT RIGHT."
—MUDDY WATERS

Muddy's fresh sound caught the attention of two brothers. They owned a record company that would later become Chess Records. In 1947, Muddy recorded an album with the brothers. The feeling and **intensity** in Muddy's voice gripped listeners. Some of the album's songs became popular, especially with people from the South. In 1948, his song "Rollin' Stone" was a smash hit.

Muddy Waters performing for fans

"PEOPLE SHOULD HEAR THE PURE BLUES—THE BLUES WE USED TO HAVE WHEN WE HAD NO MONEY."
—MUDDY WATERS

In the 1950s, Muddy recorded more albums and more hit songs. These included "I'm Ready." He played with other blues musicians. And Muddy **mentored** new talent, such as Buddy Guy. Muddy toured the United States and Europe. He played concerts and festivals around the world.

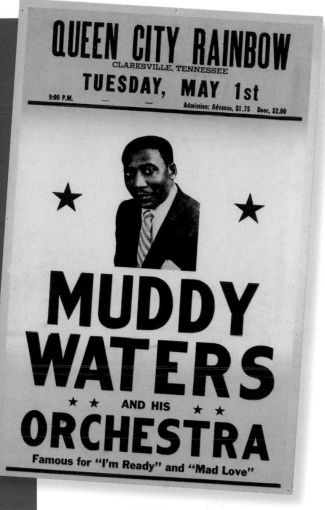

One of Muddy's concert posters

At a 1958 concert in England, Muddy said, "I was definitely too loud for them." There was a headline in the next morning's paper. It said Muddy played with a "Screaming Guitar!"

By the 1960s, Muddy's music was less popular. However, he kept putting on great shows. In 1960, Muddy performed at the Newport Jazz Festival in Rhode Island. One **critic** said Muddy "lays it down tough and cool." The audience danced as Muddy sang his heart out. The performance was recorded as one of the first live blues albums.

Muddy's powerful music always captured his Southern upbringing.

"I WAS JUST LIKE THAT, LIKE A ROLLIN' STONE."
—MUDDY WATERS

Many musicians inspired by Muddy's electric blues formed rock bands. These bands included the Rolling Stones, Cream, and Fleetwood Mac. The musicians often covered Muddy's songs. Muddy later said, "The blues had a baby and they called it rock and roll."

A Rolling Stones album cover

The Rolling Stones named their band after Muddy's song "Rollin' Stone." "When you listen to Muddy Waters, you can hear all of the angst and all of the power . . . that made that man," said Keith Richards of the Rolling Stones.

MUDDY'S IMPACT

In the 1970s, Muddy toured with rock and roller Eric Clapton from Cream. Many thousands of mostly white rock fans got to hear Muddy perform. During this time, Muddy received many awards. He earned six Grammys. In 1978, Muddy said, "This is the best point in my life." He continued, "I'm glad it came before I died."

In the 1980s, Muddy struggled with health problems. On April 30, 1983, he died in his sleep at age 68. Some of the world's most famous musicians attended his **funeral**. Today, Muddy is remembered for sharing the blues with the world—and for changing the history of music. "What Muddy Waters did for us is what we should do for others," Keith Richards said. "He passed it on."

"I BEEN IN THE BLUES ALL MY LIFE. I'M STILL DELIVERING 'CAUSE I GOT A LONG MEMORY."
—MUDDY WATERS

Muddy Waters became a part of the Rock and Roll Hall of Fame in 1987.

Muddy married twice. He had four children, two of whom became blues singers.

GREATEST HITS

Here are some of Muddy Waters's signature songs:

Baby, Please Don't Go

Still a Fool

Rollin' Stone

Mannish Boy

Country Blues

I'm a King Bee

Got My Mojo Working

Rollin' and Tumblin'

Trouble No More

You Need Love

GLOSSARY

amplifier (AM-pluh-fahy-er) a device that makes instruments louder

critic (KRIT-ik) a person who judges something

distinctive (dih-STINGK-tiv) having a special quality

funeral (FYOO-nuh-ruhl) a ceremony that is held after a person dies

grueling (GROO-uh-ling) very hard, difficult, or tiring

idol (EYE-duhl) a hero; a person whom others look up to and respect

intensity (in-TEN-suh-tee) a high level of action and effort

juke joints (JOOK JOINTS) a place where people meet up to listen to music

legacy (LEG-uh-see) anything handed down from the past

mentored (MEN-tawrd) advised

migration (mye-GRAY-shuhn) a journey from one place to another

opportunities (op-er-TOO-nih-teez) chances that make something possible

plantation (plan-TAY-shuhn) a large farm where workers grow crops, such as cotton

racism (RAY-siz-uhm) a system of beliefs and policies based on the idea that one race or group of people is better than another

segregated (SEG-ruh-gay-tid) separated from others, especially Black people from white people

sharecropper (SHAIR-krop-er) a farmer who pays as rent a share of the crop to the landowner

terrorized (TER-uh-rahyzd) created extreme fear and distress

FIND OUT MORE

BOOKS

Levy, Joel. *Turn It Up! A Pitch-Perfect History of Music That Rocked the World*. Washington, DC: National Geographic Kids, 2019.

Mahin, Michael. *Muddy: The Story of Blues Legend Muddy Waters*. New York, NY: Atheneum Books, 2017.

Richards, Mary, and David Schweitzer. *A History of Music for Children*. London, UK: Thames & Hudson, 2021.

WEBSITES

Explore these online sources with an adult:

Britannica Kids: Muddy Waters

Grammy Awards: Muddy Waters

Mojo Museum: Muddy Waters

INDEX

ABOUT THE AUTHOR

Joyce Markovics has written hundreds of books for kids. She appreciates the power of music to move and unite us. Joyce is grateful to all people who have beaten the odds to tell their stories and make great art. She would like to deeply thank Michael Kramer for his help with this book series.